Making
Knitted
Animals

Hawthorn Press

First published in Denmark in 2005 by Forlaget Olivia, under the title
Strikkede dyr © Olivia, Copenhagen 2005.

Anne-Dorthe Grigaff is hereby identified as author of this work in accordance with Section 77 of the Copyright, Designs and Patent Act, 1988. She asserts and gives notice of her moral right under this Act.

Published by Hawthorn Press, Hawthorn House, 1 Lansdown Lane,
Stroud, Gloucestershire, GL5 1BJ, UK
Tel: (01453) 757040 Email: info@hawthornpress.com

Hawthorn Press
www.hawthornpress.com

English edition *Knitted Animals* © Hawthorn Press 2006
First edition ISBN: 978-1-903458-68-6
Translated by Irena Tully, www.impulsefilms.com
Photographs by Bjarni B. Jacobsen
Book design by Anne-Dorthe Grigaff

Republished as a second edition 2023
Cover design and typesetting by Lucy Guenot
Printed by Micropress Printers Ltd, Suffolk
Printed on environmentally friendly paper from sustainable forest stock
With thanks to Solspejlet, Frederiksborggade 41, 1360 Copenhagen K., Denmark, for kindly lending the wooden toys photographed in this book.

British Library Cataloguing in Publication Data applied for
ISBN 978-1-912480-85-2

Making
Knitted
Animals

Anne-Dorthe Grigaff

Hawthorn Press

Contents

Foreword

Making toys for children is in itself a pleasurable pastime for adults, as we can nourish parts of ourselves that we otherwise too often ignore in our busy everyday lives. This activity gives us an opportunity to withdraw and be at peace with our thoughts for a while, allowing space for a creative process.

In knitted animals made by parents or grandparents, both love and joy are woven together like invisible material. Consequently this gift, this special toy, will be received differently from one that can be replaced just by returning to the shop.

Of course, a small cat or other knitted animal can come apart or be misplaced, but there is something especially comforting about getting a 'little sister cat' for the one that has been lost. Maybe the child has been fortunate enough to see how the toy was made. The amazement at what adults can create with their skilled hands will make the pleasure all the greater and the grief easier to bear.

Many of the models are so easy to knit that older children, too, can make them – especially with some grown-up help to give a hand.

At school one day I met a father who told me that his 10-year-old son was a keen knitter and very much enjoyed knitting when he got up in the mornings. He did not watch children's TV programmes like other children, and the father admitted that he found it a bit strange to see his son sitting there knitting. It struck me that this child had probably found a reflective, peaceful space, and a creative activity he enjoyed. We talked a little more about why it is good for children to knit. Afterwards the father saw how knitting could benefit the boy, and was more understanding – even proud.

A good time for children to learn to knit is around seven years of age, when their motor skills can cope with the challenge. The child learns by imitating the adult. At the school where I work, the 14 to 15-year-old pupils are invited to team up with pupils aged 7-8 years. The older pupils sit the younger ones on their lap and show them how to knit. In this way younger pupils quickly learn how to knit and at the same time form a social bond with the older ones, who are flattered by the confidence the younger children show in their abilities.

In learning to knit the child also practises coordination, fine-tunes motor skills and uses logical thinking. Modern brain researchers and neurobiologists confirm that practical abilities and cognitive skills are learned through the body: grasping things with the hands forms the basis for later grasping things with the mind too. But quite apart from technical abilities, learning to knit also develops a child's sense of aesthetics and beauty.

The wonderful thing about teaching children to knit at an early age is that their senses are so open and they find it so natural to learn through the body. They are still at the stage where they want to do the things they see adults doing. They gain great pleasure from making things that are handy and useful, especially as small gifts for the family. It is important to find activities appropriate for the age of the child, and small objects that are fun to play with, like those in this book. Several of them are little more than a square that forms the basis for a small animal. Initially the adult can sew the animal together, although very soon the child will want to do it on his or her own. By all means let the child do so, and help only when it is absolutely necessary. Children will be very proud when they see what a simple little square can be made into. There is added mystery in the flat shape transforming into a rounded shape. Of course, you do not need to explain all this to children; just let them experience it and thrill to life's mysteries. Later on the experience can be recalled in geometry.

An old Chinese proverb says: 'Show me and I see, tell me and I remember, involve me and I understand.'

Consider, also, that knitting brings the child into close contact with the yarn and the knitting needles. Give the child the best, preferably natural materials. This provides a good sensory experience and teaches the child, for instance, about the warmth-giving qualities of wool or the cooling qualities of flax and cotton. I think it is best to start with wool, however, because it is more flexible and easier for the child to work with. It smells wonderful and if you opt for wooden knitting needles the child gets a good, versatile needle that offers less resistance than metal needles.

At the school where I work we recite the following verse before we start teaching the smaller pupils:

'Train your hands
Make busy your arms
Practice the clear power of thought
With the warm-heartedness of art
In your hand sleeps the spirit'

Much wisdom lies hidden in this verse. As an adult I often marvel at it, because it formulates succinctly what would otherwise take many words to explain.

Have fun knitting with your child!

Anne-Dorthe Grigaff

Materials & techniques

See also the Glossary (page 60) for needle sizes and explanation of stitches.

Yarns

The materials are as natural as can be. When children encounter natural materials, their sensory experience is enhanced. As a rule I mix two different types of yarn in order to achieve the best possible colour and surface structure. This gives a living surface that is much more animal-like. Often wool is mixed with silk, or a bouclé yarn with a smooth yarn. Knitting is also a touch faster with two yarns, making it easier to form the animal. Once you have discovered this method, the possibilities are endless. Leftover yarns gain a new lease of life, and even the yarns from old, discarded sweaters can be reused. Aim to use yarns or combinations of yarns that reflect the colours and characteristics of each animal, and select the needle size accordingly. All these patterns can also be knitted using single yarns, which may be more suitable for new and inexperienced knitters. If you knit with a single yarn, the yarn packaging will indicate the appropriate size. As a rough guide, use 3 to 3.25mm (US2–4) with 4 ply, 4mm (US6) with double knit or doubled 4 ply and 4.5 to 5mm (US7–8) with chunky or doubled double knit. Choice of yarn and needle size can also be exploited to vary the scale of the animals.

Stuffing

The animals can be stuffed with wool, but for people who are allergic to wool it may be necessary to use another material e.g. web of carded cotton fibres, kapok or something similar. You should also keep allergy issues in mind when choosing yarns.

Knitting needles

I use wooden needles which enhance the pleasure of knitting. They become smoother with time, more beautiful, and using them is beneficial if one is prone to sore joints, since they are more 'springy'.

Charts

Diagrams make it easier to work the more complicated shapes. Read the charts from the bottom working up to the top.

Mother duck with her ducklings

Materials

- Duck-coloured yarn. A double-knit mohair and white alpaca can be used, which makes the duck really soft
- Needle size: as appropriate for yarn used
- Carded wool for stuffing

The eyes are sewn on in a black or dark colour. The beak is sewn using left-over orange woollen yarn.

Mother duck

BODY: cast on 30 stitches and work 20 rows in garter stitch. Cast off loosely.

HEAD: cast on 16 stitches and work 12 rows in garter stitch. Cast off.

Ducklings

BODY: cast on 15 stitches and work 10 rows in garter stitch. Cast off.

HEAD: cast on 8 stitches and work 6 rows in garter stitch. Cast off.

To make up:

BODY: fold the body lengthwise and sew it together at the top and sides, leaving the bottom edge open for stuffing. Make sure that the body rounds out nicely at the corners. Make the tail end pointed when sewing it together. Stuff with wool so the body becomes firm and oval-shaped with a pointed tail. Sew bottom edge.

HEAD: fold the head and sew it together. Make it as round as possible. Stuff it with wool and sew it onto the body.

BEAK: make the beak out of left-over orange woollen yarn. Sew it in overlapping buttonhole stitch so a round duck-like beak emerges.

EYES: sew in dark yarn, approximately 2-3 stitches.

1

cast off

HEAD
M: 12 rows
D: 6 rows

MOTHER: cast on 16 stitches
DUCKLING: cast on 8 stitches

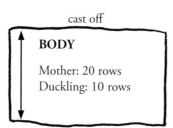

cast off

BODY

Mother: 20 rows
Duckling: 10 rows

MOTHER: cast on 30 stitches
DUCKLING: cast on 15 stitches

2

sew

sew

fold

HEAD

sew

sew

fold

BODY

3

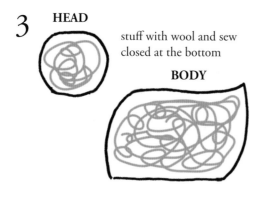

HEAD

stuff with wool and sew closed at the bottom

BODY

4

sew the eyes with dark yarn

sew the head on firmly

make the beak with orange yarn

Sweet, soft little ducklings that quack after mother and find their place in line. It's fun feeding the ducks and watching them rush after the food (sweetcorn, peas, rice or oats – rather than bread) you give them. Lovely toys for young park visitors.

Growly bear with big paws

Materials

- Hairy effect yarn
- Tweed yarn
- Needle size: 3.5mm (US4)
- Carded wool for stuffing
- Dark pearl yarn for the eyes and nose

The yarn I have used here is very hairy effect yarn of wool and mohair mixed with a tweed yarn to give good close knitting. The bear is knitted on 3.5mm needles to achieve the tightest knitting possible. The long 'bear fur' must be fished out with a knitting needle or needle, so that as much fur as possible is on the outside. Start at the back and knit towards the nose. Then continue knitting to make the bear's under-side. The bear is knitted all in one piece (stocking stitch) except for the ears (garter stitch).

BODY: cast on 16 stitches. Starting with a purl row work in stocking stitch. Increase 1 stitch at either end of the 2nd row (18sts). Work the 3rd row with no shaping (purl).

BACK LEGS: Cast on 10 stitches at the beginning of the 4th and 5th rows. Now you have begun to knit the back legs.
Increase 2 stitches at the centre of the 6th row to form the bear's spinal column. It should bend upwards a little where the hip is. At this point you should have 40 stitches on your needle. Work 4 rows. Finish the shaping for the back legs by casting off 10 stitches at the beginning of the 10th and 11th rows. Decrease 2 stitches in the centre of the 12th row (18 stitches remain) so that the spinal column now bends downwards. Work 4 rows for the tummy.
SHOULDERS: Cast on 10 stitches at the beginning of the 16th and 17th rows, and increase by 2 stitches at the centre of the 18th row for the bear's shoulders.
NECK: Knit 3 rows. Cast off 12 stitches at the beginning of the 22nd and 23rd rows for the neck, and decrease by 2 stitches at the centre of the work. At this point you should have 14 stitches on your needle.

NECK AND HEAD: work 1–2 rows. The last row should be a purl row. Work the next row as follows: knit 1 stitch, knit 2 together, knit 3, knit 2 together, knit 3, knit 2 together, knit 1. (11 sts)

Work 2 rows without shaping. On the following row decrease 1 stitch at the beginning and end of the row. (9 sts)

Work 2 rows. On the following knit row: knit 1 stitch, increase 1 stitch, knit 2, increase 1 stitch, knit 2, increase 1 stitch, knit 1. Purl 1 row. (12sts)

Next knit row: knit 3, increase 1 stitch, knit 4, increase 1 stitch, knit 3. (14sts)

Work 2 rows.

The purl row: purl 3, decrease 1 stitch, purl 4, decrease 1 stitch, purl 3. (12 sts)

Work 2 rows.

The knit row: knit 3, decrease 1 stitch, knit 3, decrease 1 stitch, knit 2. (10 sts)

Work 2 rows.

The purl row: purl 2, purl 2 stitches together, 3 times altogether, purl 1.

Work 2 rows.

The knit row: knit 1, decrease 1 stitch, knit 2, decrease 1 stitch. (5sts)

Purl 1 row.

Knit 2 stitches together 2 times. (3 sts remain).

THE UNDERSIDE: work 3 rows. On the following row: increase 1 stitch at the beginning and end of the row. (5 sts). Work 8 rows. Once again, increase 1 stitch at the beginning and end of the following row. (7 sts) Work 9 rows.

Repeat on the following row, increasing at the beginning and end of the row. (9sts)

TUMMY: cast on 6 stitches at either end of the next row. Work 6 rows. (21sts) Cast off 6 stitches at the beginning and end of the next row for each leg and work 6 rows (9 sts). Cast on 6 stitches at either end of the next row for the back legs. On the next 2 rows, decrease 1 stitch at the centre of the work. Work a further 4 rows.

EARS: cast on 5 stitches and work 3 rows in garter stitch. Cast off 1 stitch at the beginning of the next 2 rows. Cast off the last 3 stitches. Work the other ear exactly the same.

To make up:

Sew the underside to the upper body. The underside is somewhat smaller, so you may need to stretch it to fit. Leave the rear open so that you can stuff the bear with wool until it is firm and begins to take shape. You will probably need to shape the body a little after it has been stuffed, using a needle and thread. Add a few stitches in the body and head, or wherever you think the bear needs a bit more shape. Use pearl yarn or embroidery thread to sew some small eyes and a nose.

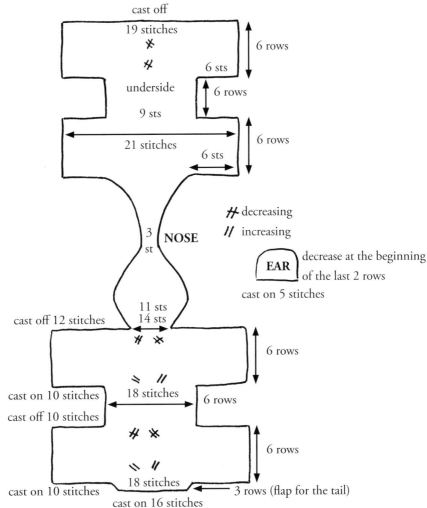

cast off
19 stitches
underside
9 sts
21 stitches
6 rows
6 sts
6 rows
6 rows
6 sts

3 st   NOSE

decreasing
// increasing

EAR   decrease at the beginning of the last 2 rows
cast on 5 stitches

11 sts
14 sts
cast off 12 stitches

cast on 10 stitches   18 stitches   6 rows
cast off 10 stitches   6 rows

6 rows
18 stitches
cast on 10 stitches   3 rows (flap for the tail)
cast on 16 stitches

Sheep and lamb's wool is so soft and warm. Lovely and cosy to cuddle up with.

Soft sheep & lamb

Materials

- Mohair-bouclé or other wool bouclé
- Needle size: to suit yarn used
- Carded wool for stuffing
- Crochet hook

There are three possible sizes, with the middle size shown in brackets.

BODY: cast on 36 (24) 18 stitches and work in garter stitch until you have 10 (8) 6 rows. Cast off 8 (6) 4 stitches at the beginning and end of the next row, breaking and rejoining the yarn as necessary. Work a further 10 (8) 6 rows. Cast on 8 (6) 4 stitches at either end of the next row. Work 10 (8) 6 rows and decrease by casting off 12 (8) 4 stitches at either end of the next row. Work 24 (16) 12 rows. Cast off.

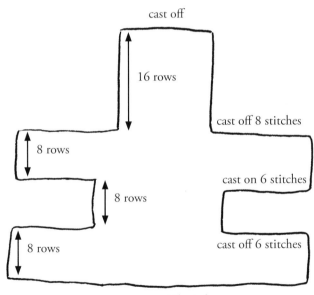

cast off

16 rows

cast off 8 stitches

8 rows

8 rows

cast on 6 stitches

cast off 6 stitches

8 rows

cast on e.g.24 stitches

To make up:

Sew the legs and tummy together. Leave the rear of the sheep open for stuffing.

Roll the wool into a firm 'sausage' and press it down into the leg. Do the same with the other legs.

You can roll the wool tightly around a knitting needle, or narrow pointed scissors, and press it down into the leg. Press the knitting needle/scissors with your right hand, while holding the leg with your left hand. While the right hand is stuffing, the left hand is shaping. Don't stuff the head and tummy too hard.

Sew the rear of the sheep together. Crochet the tail as a row of chain stitches. Shape the ears using a short row of chain stitches and sew them to each side of the head with several stitches.

Make the ears with a crochet chain.

Sew the legs into a long 'tube' and sew them together at the head and tail. Fill the tummy with wool and sew it together.

Teddy bear

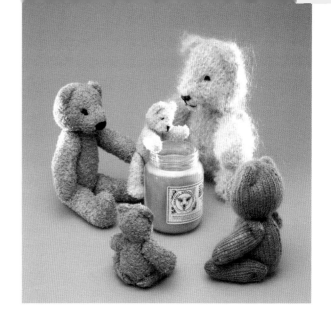

Materials

- Approx. 100g (4 oz) mohair bouclé
- Needle size: 3.5mm (US4) and a long doll's needle
- Carded wool for stuffing
- Black pearl yarn for the nose (pearl yarn is mercerised cotton, which is slightly glossy)

BODY AND HEAD: begin with the head. Cast on 35 stitches. Work in stocking stitch to a length of 9cm (3¾in). Decrease 10 stitches evenly spaced along the next row. Continue until the body measures 20cm (7½in), finishing with a purl row. Decrease 5 stitches evenly spaced over the next row. (20 stitches on your needle) Work 3 rows. Decrease 5 stitches on the next row as before. Purl 1 row. Decrease 5 stitches on the next row. Purl 1 row. Decrease 5 stitches in the next row. Cast off the remaining 5 stitches.
ARMS: cast on 14 stitches. Work in stocking stitch until the work measures approx. 11cm (4¼in), finishing with a purl row. Decrease on the next row as follows: knit 2 stitches together, knit 1, knit 2 stitches together. Purl

1 row. Decrease again on the next row as before. Cast off.
LEGS: cast on 14 stitches. Work in stocking stitch until the work measures 8cm (3¼in), finishing with a purl row. Cast on 3 stitches at the start of the next 2 rows. Purl 1 row. Increase 1 stitch at each end of the next row. Work 4 rows. Decrease 1 stitch at each end of the purl row. Cast off knitwise.
NOSE: cast on 14 stitches. Work in stocking stitch to produce a square. Cast off.

To make up:

BODY AND HEAD: sew up the seam of the body and the head. Avoid sewing all the way down, as there has to be an opening for the wool stuffing. Turn inside out. The bear looks nicest with the wrong side out as it is not as 'stripy' as the plain side.

Roll a firm ball of wool into the head part, about the size of a tennis ball. Tighten well around the ball and make sure that it is a nice, harmonious round shape. Mould the wool a little, as it does not matter if there is a small 'tail' on the ball. You can push it down into the neck part. Tie around the neck with a double thread (the same thread). Fill the body with the wool and sew it together. Shape the body until it is oblong, well-proportioned and firm.

You may need more wool. It requires practice to stuff the bear. If it is not tightly stuffed, it quickly becomes too floppy.

Sew together at the bottom and fasten the yarn by sewing it in and out of the bear. The wool stuffing helps to prevent the fastening coming undone. Pull the ears forward a little and sew them into shape without stuffing with wool.

NOSE: sew the nose on like a 'clown nose' – a little bit loosely so it is baggy. Leave the last side open for stuffing. Roll another firm ball and stuff it in. Sew the last side firmly. Shape the nose a little so it looks cute.

HEAD

BODY

sew together

EAR

opening for wool stuffing

wool

place a woollen ball in the nose and sew it firmly

NOSE

sew the arms and legs together, fill with wool and sew the rest together

sew the eyes and mouth with black pearl yarn

sew the arms and legs firmly onto the body with strong cotton yarn

LEGS AND ARMS: sew the seams of the legs and arms together so that they are open at the top. Fill with wool little by little, again very firmly. Both legs should be the same thickness and the feet the same size with the same amount of stuffing.

Sew the arms together and stuff them in the same way. Sew up the top.

SEW THE LEGS AND ARMS TO THE BODY: (see drawing) you will need a 'good eye' so the arms don't look as if they are growing out of the neck. They must be at shoulder height. Stick the long needle through the body and hang the legs or arms on it. Find a good position and don't sew the seams until you are satisfied.

Sew from the inside of the legs/arms through the body towards the other leg/arm. Tighten the thread. Sew the other way back and tighten afterwards so the arms/legs are joined firmly and tightly to the body. Sew a couple of times back and forth. Then the legs and arms can move up and down.

NOSE AND MOUTH: Using the black pearl yarn sew round the end of the nose until you have a nice triangular shape. Sew on a line for the mouth.

EYES: place the eyes right over the snout. It's a matter of taste how close the eyes should be to each other. Use a couple of pins of the same colour to mark where the eyes should be. They must sit right beside each other and must be sewn many times back and forth through the eyes in order to be visible. They can be round or square according to taste.

Now the teddy is ready for a hug.

Giving a silky-soft cat which you have made is the nicest gift imaginable for a child.

Clever, playful cats

Materials

- Alpaca wool
- Mohair yarn
- 2 colours of angora or other hairy yarn (you can also use home-spun yarn which can be brushed up afterwards)
- Needle size: to suit yarn used
- Carded wool for stuffing
- A bit of pearl yarn for the eyes and the nose (if the cat is light coloured, blue eyes and a pink nose are nice. Otherwise black pearl yarn is best)

The size depends on how thick the yarn is and on the size of the needle. You can reduce the number of stitches according to the size you want. Just follow these rules:

- the body is always square
- the head is 2 squares long
- the tail is 2/3 of the body length

BODY: start e.g. with 24 stitches: work in stocking stitch to form a square. Cast off.
HEAD: cast on 12 stitches. Work in stocking stitch until you have a square. Measure and work the same number of rows again so it is twice as long. Cast off.
TAIL: cast on 6 stitches and work 2/3 of the body length. Cast off.

To make up:

Fold the corners of the body towards each other so you have four new corners, or paws (see below). Join the seams with overcast stitch until there is a little open hole in the middle. Fill it with wool, form the body and sew it together under the tummy. The wool must be pressed well into the paws.

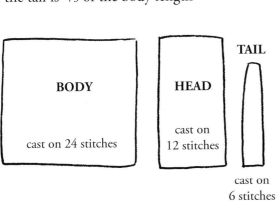

BODY cast on 24 stitches

HEAD cast on 12 stitches

TAIL cast on 6 stitches

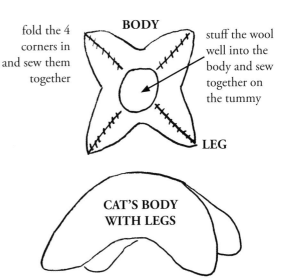

fold the 4 corners in and sew them together

BODY

stuff the wool well into the body and sew together on the tummy

LEG

CAT'S BODY WITH LEGS

Fold the head in the middle and sew up the sides, so a little 'bag' is created. Roll a woollen ball for stuffing the head, and roll another ball for a nose. Gather the head into the neck and sew it firmly onto the body. Pull the head up a little where the ears will be. Sew them into shape. Add eyes, nose and mouth using the pearl yarn.

Sew up the tail. Stuff it with a little bit of wool and sew it firmly onto the body so it bends straight up.
Put a bow around the neck with a little bell. Older children will love that. Young children can choke on bells, so it is not suitable for children under 3.

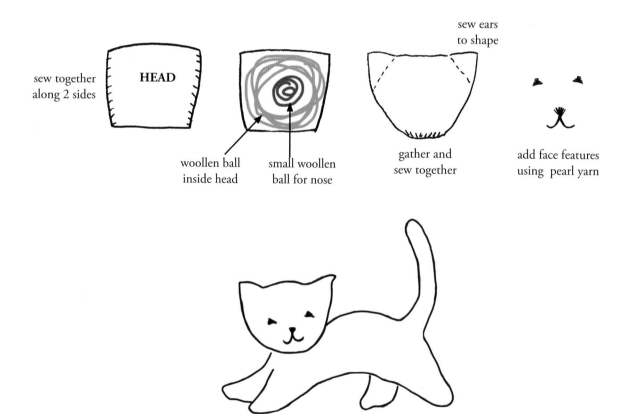

sew ears
to shape

sew together
along 2 sides

HEAD

woollen ball
inside head

small woollen
ball for nose

gather and
sew together

add face features
using pearl yarn

Mischievous dogs

Materials

- Mohair bouclé in a good doggy colour Mohair yarn
- Needle size: 4.5mm (US7)
- Carded wool for stuffing
- A bit of pearl yarn for the nose, mouth and eyes

BODY: cast on 26 stitches. Work 10 rows of stocking stitch. Cast off 6 stitches for each leg at the beginning and end of the next row, breaking and rejoining the yarn as necessary. Work 6 rows of stocking stitch on the remaining 14 stitches and then cast on another 6 stitches at either end of the next row for the legs. Work 10 rows of stocking stitch and cast off.

HEAD: cast on 14 stitches. Work 2 rows of stocking stitch. Increase 1 stitch at the beginning and end of each knit row, 3 times altogether until there are 20 stitches. Finish with a purl row. Work 4 rows of stocking stitch and cast off.

EARS: cast on 5 stitches and work 3 rows. Start with a purl row. On the 4th row, knit the first and last 2 stitches together. Purl 1 row and cast off. Repeat with the other ear.

TAIL: cast on 6 stitches and work 15 rows of stocking stitch. Cast off 2 stitches at the beginning of the 16th and 17th rows. Purl the next row. Cast off.

They can be cheeky, they can be cuddly, they can get up to naughty tricks, and yet they are always a loyal friend who understands exactly how you feel.

To make up:

Sew the legs together. Sew the dog's front and rear parts together, gathering the seams as you go. Leave an opening in the middle for the wool stuffing. Roll some wool tightly like a 'sausage' around pointed scissors and push it down into the leg. Hold the wool while you're pulling the scissors out. Repeat with the other leg. Roll a thick woollen 'sausage' for the body and push it in. Sew the dog together under the tummy. Sew the head together, start at the top of the head and progress towards the nose and then from the nose towards the neck. Stuff with wool until the head is firm, and sew it onto the body. Sew the ears on and fold them in the desired position. You can sew the nose and eyes in position by sewing into the wool and tightening the thread a little. Sew the tail together and stuff it just like the legs. Sew it firmly to the rear of the body.

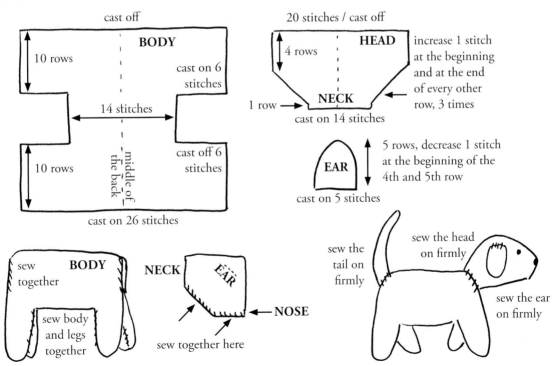

Squirrel

Materials

- Mohair yarn, a thin woollen yarn and silk tweed. Together these three yarns give a good structure. Silk tweed gives good nuanced and frizzy knitting, and the mohair provides volume. The thin woollen yarn adds volume
- Needle size: 3mm (US2–3)
- Carded wool for stuffing

BODY: cast on 20 stitches. Work 42 rows of stocking stitch. Cast off loosely.

HEAD: cast on 14 stitches. Work 8 rows. Cast off.

EARS: cast on 5 stitches. Work 2 rows. Decrease 1 stitch at the beginning of each row until 1 stitch remains. Break the yarn and pull it through the last stitch.

To make up:

BODY: sew the body together in the same way as the cat on page 25, but the squirrel's back legs must be bigger than the front legs. Sew a little between the legs so they point the right way.

HEAD: fold the knitted piece and sew it together at the top and along one side. Gather it a little at the top so it is as round as possible – but the pointed part at the highest corner of the side must be pointed. That will be the nose. Stuff with wool until it feels nice and firm. Gather at the neck and sew the head firmly onto the body. It is absolutely necessary to shape the squirrel's head some more before you sew on the eyes and nose. Place the ears high and close together on the head.

TAIL: make this in the same way as the fox tail on page 46. The tail must be approximately as long as the squirrel's body and there must be space for it to bend a little. Sew it firmly and shape it so it has the right squirrel look.

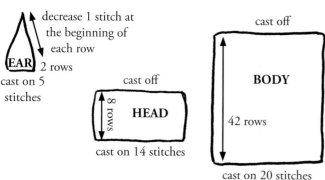

decrease 1 stitch at the beginning of each row

EAR 2 rows

cast on 5 stitches

cast off

HEAD 8 rows

cast on 14 stitches

cast off

BODY 42 rows

cast on 20 stitches

Goosey Lucy

from a story called Kluck *by the brothers Grimm*

Materials

- Goose-coloured yarn (a combination of a natural coloured Shetland wool and a white and beige silk bouclé could be used)
- Needle size: to suit yarn used
- Carded wool for stuffing
- Black wool yarn for the eyes, yellow/orange woollen yarn for the beak and the feet

BACK BODY: cast on 4 stitches and work 2 rows garter stitch. Begin increasing for the body – increase 1 stitch at the beginning and end of the next row. Work 1 row and repeat, increasing on every other row until there are 24 stitches (21 rows).

NECK: Work 12 rows. Begin decreasing for the neck by knitting 2 stitches together at the beginning and end of every other row until there are 10 stitches left.

Work a further 12 rows on the neck until there are 58 rows in total.

HEAD: Increase 3 stitches on the next row, 1 at either end and 1 in the centre. Work another 6 rows and cast off.

BREAST PART: cast on 2 stitches. Work 3 rows.(Increase at the beginning and end of the next row, and knit 4 rows) twice. (Increase at the beginning and end of the next row, and knit 3 rows) twice. Increase at the beginning and end of the next row (12 stitches altogether). Continue without shaping until there are 36 rows. Begin decreasing at the beginning and end of every other row until there are 2 stitches left. Cast off.

FEET: using yellow/orange yarn, cast on 2 stitches. Knit 1 row. Increase 1 stitch at each end of the next row. Work 5 rows and increase 1 stitch at each end of the next row (6 stitches). Work 5 rows. Make the toes in the next row: wool forward/around the needle, knit 2 stitches together (through front of stitches), 3 times altogether (6 stitches remain). Work 5 rows. Decrease 1 stitch at each end of the next row. Work 5 rows and decrease another stitch at each end of the next row. Knit 1 row and cast off. Work the other foot in the same way.

To make up:

Sew the head and neck together to about the middle of the neck. Sew the head together so it is nice and round.

Pin the breast gusset firmly in place and sew it on. Stuff the body with wool before you sew it together completely. Stuff it firmly so it is easier to shape. Sew the last opening together and begin shaping.

Bend the head down a little and sew under the chin. Bend the neck backwards a little and sew in the back of the neck. Keep adjusting the tail and back until you are satisfied with the shape. Sew the beak in overlapping buttonhole stitch

until it is long and round. Fold the feet in half and sew the edges together. Sew the feet on with buttonhole stitch. It stiffens them so they stand better. You can sew little furrows between the toes to stiffen them even more. Sew the feet firmly onto the body. Stitch the eyes with a dark coloured woollen yarn.

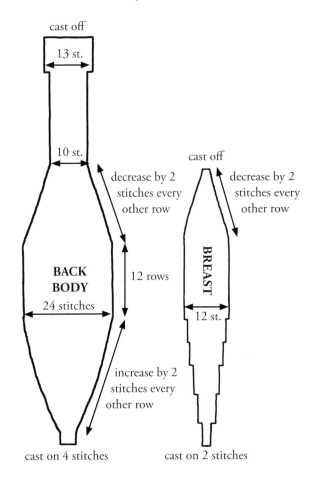

Hoppy the hare

Materials

- Angora and kid mohair is used here, as for the cuddly bunny on page 40. See the reference regarding yarn on facing page.
- Needle size: to suit yarn used
- Carded wool for stuffing
- Black wool yarn for the eyes and nose

BODY AND HEAD: knitted in one piece. Cast on 20 stitches and work in garter stitch until there are 32 rows. Cast off.
EARS: cast on 5 stitches and work 20 rows. On the next row knit the 2nd and the 3rd stitches together. Knit 1 row and repeat, decreasing twice more. Cast off the last 2 stitches.
TAIL: cast on 8 stitches and work 7 rows. Cast off.

To make up:

Sew the body together so the rows run from side to side. Make a firm little ball of wool and put it in the body. This will be the hare's head. Gather and stitch the neck and then fill the body with wool until it is good and firm. Sew the body together at the bottom. Sew the ears firmly onto the head. Make a little woollen ball and place it in the sewn-together part for the tail. Sew the tail onto the hare. You can sew the eyes and nose on discreetly, but it is not always necessary. The hare has its own expression, enhanced by the long ears, and most children will recognise it instantly, with or without a nose and eyes.

cast off

32 rows

BODY

cast on 20 stitches

knit the 2nd and the 3rd stitch together on every 2nd row

EAR 20 rows

cast on 5 stitches

cast off

7 rows **TAIL**

cast on 8 stitches

Any yarn with an appropriate hare-colour can
be used here. As a rule I use two
different types of yarn, which gives the
best colour structure and surface.
The result is more lively than if you
only use one type of yarn. In addition,
knitting is also a touch faster and the
animal is also easier to shape.
This model is very simple and is well
suited for children to knit.
Younger knitters may need some
help to sew and stuff the hare if
they have not tried it before.

1
Fold the body piece in half and sew up the sides.

2
Sew the top closed making a rounded top for the head.

3
Stuff a woollen ball inside the head.

4
Gather in at the neck

5
Fill the body with wool and sew it closed at the bottom.

6
Sew the ears firmly on to the head.

7
Sew on a mouth, nose and eyes.

8
Sew the tail together and gather it at the bottom. Put a little woollen ball in and sew the tail firmly onto the body.

Harry the horse

Materials
- Two balls of mohair yarn and angora wool
- Needle size: to suit yarn used
- Carded wool for stuffing
- Black pearl yarn for the eyes
- Yarn for the mane and tail

BODY: cast on 40 stitches and work in garter stitch until there are 12 rows.

Cast off 11 stitches at the beginning and end of the next row, breaking and rejoining the yarn as necessary. Work 14 rows.

Cast on 11 stitches at either end of the next row. Knit 20 stitches, turn the work and cast on 11 stitches in one go. Turn back and continue knitting (51 sts). This will make a hole which will be sewn together later.

Knit 1 row over the newly cast-on stitches and knit to the end of the row. On alternate rows, pick up 1 stitch before and after the middle stitch (29 sts).

Work 12 rows and start shaping for the front legs. Cast off 20 stitches at the beginning and end of the next row.

Work 2 rows on the remaining 19 stitches. Cast on 3 stitches at either end of the next row and then 1 stitch at either end of the next 2 rows (29 sts). Work 6 rows. Decrease 1 stitch at each end of the next row and cast off.

EARS: cast on 5 stitches. Work 6 rows and then keep knitting the 2 middle stitches together until 1 stitch remains. Break the yarn and pull it through the last stitch.

To make up:

Sew the legs together.
Sew the head and the 'hole' at the back together. Stuff the head firmly with wool. Roll a woollen 'sausage' firmly around a knitting needle or something similar for the legs.
Place a 'sausage' down into each leg.

Make another rolled sausage and stuff the body. Sew the tummy together.
The horse must now have a mane and tail. Thread some contrasting yarn on a needle and stitch over your finger or a pencil along the horse's neck, fixing every other stitch firmly. Use scissors to cut along the mane then fluff it up. Cut 8 pieces of yarn approx. 10cms long. Fold in half to make a tail and sew firmly on to the horse.
Sew the ears on.

knit the 2 middle stitches together until there are no more stitches left

6 rows

cast on 5 stitches

cast off

cast off 1 stitch at beginning and end of last row

6 rows
increase 3 stitches on each side once

cast off 20 stitches

2 rows

increase 2 stitches every other row

12 rows

cast on 11 stitches

cast off 11 stitches

cast on 11 stitches in one go

18 stitches

14 rows

12 rows

cast on 40 stitches

Clippity clop, off goes the horse
with his mane and tail flying

Cuddly bunny

The bunny is knitted in rather extravagant angora and kid mohair which gives the softest look imaginable. Warning! Once you have held such a soft, cuddly bunny against your cheek you won't be able to live without it…

decrease

EAR

10 rows

cast on 7 stitches

cast off

HEAD

11 rows

cast on 22 stitches

cast off

BODY

32 rows

cast on 30 stitches

Materials

- Angora and kid mohair
- Needle size: 3mm (US2–3)
- Pink silk yarn (or pale pink stretch velour) for inner ears
- Black pearl yarn for the eyes

BODY: this is knitted almost exactly like the cat on page 25, and the squirrel on page 30. Cast on 30 stitches. Work 32 rows of stocking stitch. Cast off loosely.

HEAD: cast on 22 stitches and work 11 rows in stocking stitch. Cast off.

TAIL: cast on 12 stitches and work 6 rows in stocking stitch. Cast off.

EARS: cast on 7 stitches and work 10 rows in stocking stitch.

Decrease 1 stitch at the beginning of the next 2 rows. Work 2 rows. Repeat decreasing in the next 2 rows. Work 2 rows. Repeat decreasing in the following 2 rows and cast off.

INNER EARS: Cast on 6 stitches and work 12 rows in stocking stitch. Decrease 1 stitch at the beginning of the next 2 rows. Work 2 rows. Decrease 1 stitch at the beginning of the next 3 rows. Break the yarn and pull it through the last stitch.

To make up:

BODY: sew the body together in almost the same way as the cat on page 25, but the bunny's back legs must be bigger than its front legs. Sew a few stitches between the legs so they point the right way.

HEAD: fold and sew together at the top and along one side. Gather it together slightly at the top so it is as round as possible. But the pointed part at the side's highest corner must remain slightly pointed. This will be the nose. Stuff wool inside until it feels nice and firm. Gather together at the neck and sew the head firmly to the body. Now shape the bunny's head before you stitch the eyes and nose.

TAIL: gather the tail at the top and sew it together on the side. Stuff it with wool, gather the lowest part and sew it firmly onto the bunny.

EARS: sew the two ear parts together and place them high on the head. Before sewing the ears to the head, try folding the ears a bit and experiment with different positions until you are happy with how your bunny looks.

Chicks, hens & a cockerel

Materials

- For the chick: Light yellow yarn. Angora or alpaca wool is perfect
- For the hen: soft woollen yarn or hen-coloured cotton yarn
- For the cockerel: dark soft woollen yarn
- Orange yarn for the beaks, black for eyes
- Needle size: 3mm (US2–3)
- Carded wool for stuffing

CHICK: Cast on 10 stitches. Work a square in garter stitch, about 16 rows. Cast off. Fold the square into a triangle. Sew along one side and stuff with wool to form the body and head. Sew the last part of the chick together. Sew from the mid back to the base (see diagram on page 44) and back again to give the chick the right curve. Shape further by sewing a little here and there. Using orange yarn, sew a beak at one end. Make little eyes using dark coloured yarn.

HEN: Work the hen in the same way as the chick, just a little bigger, e.g. 24 stitches. Sew a little red comb on the head.

COCKEREL: Work the cockerel in the same way, just a bit bigger. Use rich, colourful yarn leftovers for the tail. Add 'bobbles' under the chin. The cockerel can have long legs so he can stroll around proudly in the chicken yard. You can use pipecleaners or strong copper wire wound round with the yarn or carded wool in the appropriate colour.

cast off

BODY

cast on 10 stitches for
the chick, 24 for the
hen and more for
the cockerel

fold

BODY

sew sides together

stuff the wool
through this hole

sew from the bottom up-
wards through the 'back' and
down again, then pull the yarn
so the back becomes curved

sew the
beak with
orange yarn

sew the
eye with
dark yarn

sew the 'comb' onto the
head and under the beak
with a button hole stitch

make the cockerel's
tail feathers with
colourful yarns

Fergus the fox & his cub

Materials

- Fox-coloured yarn (a combination of a terracotta red Shetland wool and an orangered silk bouclé)
- Needle size: to suit yarn used
- Carded wool for stuffing
- Natural-coloured leftover yarn for the tip of the tail
- Black pearl yarn for the eyes and nose

Large fox

BODY: cast on 30 stitches. Work in garter stitch until you have 10 rows. Cast off 5 stitches at the beginning and end of the next row (these are the back legs), breaking and rejoining the yarn as necessary.

Continue working until there are 14 rows (the body).

Cast on 5 stitches at either end of the next row. Knit 10 rows for the front legs.

Cast off 9 stitches (12 stitches remain).

Work 2 rows for the neck.

HEAD: *knit 3 stitches, pick up 1 stitch** repeat from * to ** 3 times, knit 3 stitches (15 stitches). Knit 1 row. On the next row, knit 1 stitch *pick up 1 stitch, knit 2** repeat from * to ** 7 times (22 stitches). Knit 3 rows.

Knit 7 stitches, pick up 1 stitch and knit 8, pick up 1 stitch and knit the last 7.

Knit 1 row (24 stitches).

Knit the first 7 stitches as before, pick up 1 stitch and knit 10, pick up 1 stitch and knit the last 7.

Knit the first and last 2 stitches together on the next row.

Knit 2 stitches together, knit 5, knit 2 stitches

together, knit 8, knit 2 stitches together, knit 4 and knit the last 2 stitches together (20 stitches).

In the next row, knit the first and last 2 stitches together (18 stitches).

Knit 2 stitches together, knit 2, knit 2 stitches together, knit 6, knit 2 stitches together, knit 2, knit the last 2 stitches together (14 stitches).

Knit 1 row without decreasing.

Knit 2 stitches together, knit 1, knit 2 stitches together, knit 4, knit 2 stitches together, knit 1 and knit the last 2 stitches together.

Knit 1 row without decreasing.

Knit 2 stitches together twice, knit 2, knit 2 stitches together twice. Now there should be 6 stitches left. Knit 1 row.

Knit 1 stitch, knit 2 stitches together twice, knit the last stitch.

Work 9 rows with the remaining 4 stitches. Increase 1 stitch at the beginning and end of the next row (6 stitches). Work 2 rows without shaping. Increase 1 stitch again at the beginning and end of the next row (8 stitches). Knit 1 row. Start decreasing. *Knit 2 stitches together at the beginning and end of the row (6 stitches). Knit 1 row**. Repeat from * to ** twice more and cast off.

EARS: knitting both ears separately on one needle, cast on 6 stitches. Work 3 rows in garter stitch. Decrease 1 stitch at the beginning and end of the next 2 rows. Break the yarn and pull it through the last stitch.

TAIL: take a piece of card 3 cm wide and wind a little white yarn around it for the tip of the tail, then continue winding using the same yarn as for the body. Sew with chain stitch in the middle on both sides to hold the yarn together. Pull the 'tail' off the card and sew it together in the middle to make it strong and robust. Sew it firmly, cut the loops and trim.

To make up:

Sew the legs together. Roll the wool tightly around a knitting needle or narrow pointed scissors to make four firm 'sausages', and press them down into the legs.

Press the knitting needle/scissors with one hand, while holding the leg with the other hand.

Sew the body together towards the neck and stuff it with wool in the same way as the legs. Sew the head, but leave a little gap open while you are stuffing it. The more tightly the wool

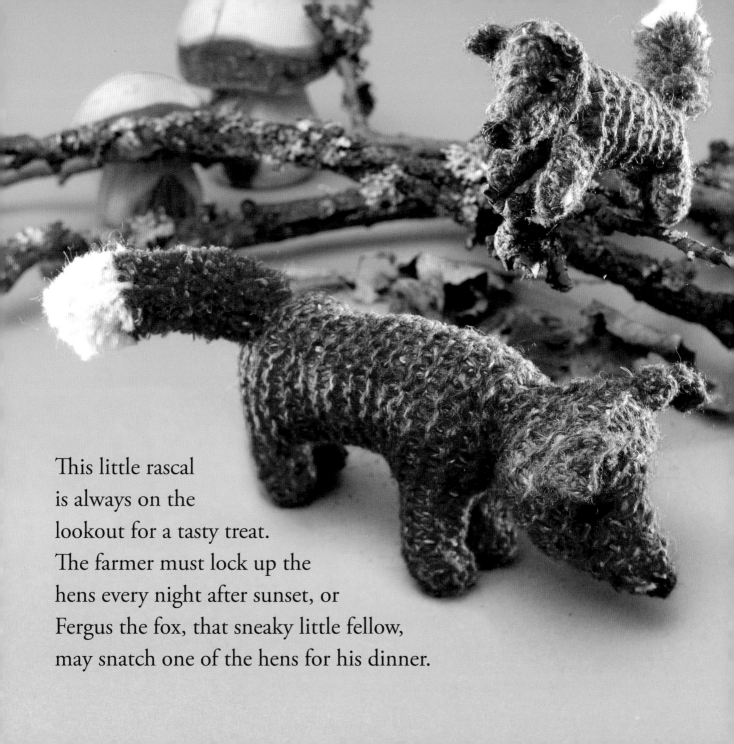

This little rascal
is always on the
lookout for a tasty treat.
The farmer must lock up the
hens every night after sunset, or
Fergus the fox, that sneaky little fellow,
may snatch one of the hens for his dinner.

is rolled before it goes down into the head, the easier it is to shape it.

Stuff the nose in the same way as the legs, to make it more pointed.

Sew the ears and tail on firmly.

Now shape the head into shape with a needle and thread. It's like modelling – pulling the head into shape with a thread which you pull through the wool. Do the same to mark the eyeholes, bridge of the nose etc.

The body also needs a loving hand. Find photographs for reference to see what a real fox looks like.

Fox cub

Cast on 20 stitches and work 5 rows. Cast off 4 stitches at the beginning and end of the next row for the leg, breaking and rejoining the yarn as necessary (12 stitches).

Work 9 rows and cast on 4 stitches at the start of the next 2 rows (20 stitches)

Work 5 rows and cast off 7 stitches at the start of the next 2 rows towards the neck (6 stitches). Knit 1 row.

HEAD: knit 2 stitches, pick up 1 stitch, knit 2, pick up 1 stitch, knit the 2 last stitches (8 stitches). Knit 1 row.

Knit 2, pick up 1 stitch, 4 times (12 stitches). Knit 1 row.

On the next row, knit 4, pick up 1 stitch, 2 times (14 stitches). Knit 2 rows.

Decrease again: knit 2 stitches, knit 2 stitches together, knit 6, knit 2 stitches together, knit 2. (12 stitches) Knit the next row.

Knit 1 stitch, knit 2 together, 4 times. (8 stitches) Knit 1 row.

Knit 2 together, 4 times. (4 stitches) Knit 1 row.

Knit 2 together twice, then knit 4 rows on the remaining 2 stitches.

NOSE: increase 1 stitch at the beginning and end of the row (now there are 4 stitches). Knit one row. Increase at each side again (6 stitches). Knit 1 row.

Decrease again: knit 2 together, knit 2, knit 2 together. (4 stitches) Knit 1 row.

Knit 2 together twice. Knit 1 row. Knit last 2 stitches together. Break the yarn and pull it through the last stitch.

To make up:

The fox cub is made up just like the adult fox. Sew the ears with buttonhole stitch in overlapping rows to make pointed fox ears.

TAIL

wind the yarn
around a piece
of card and sew
in the middle

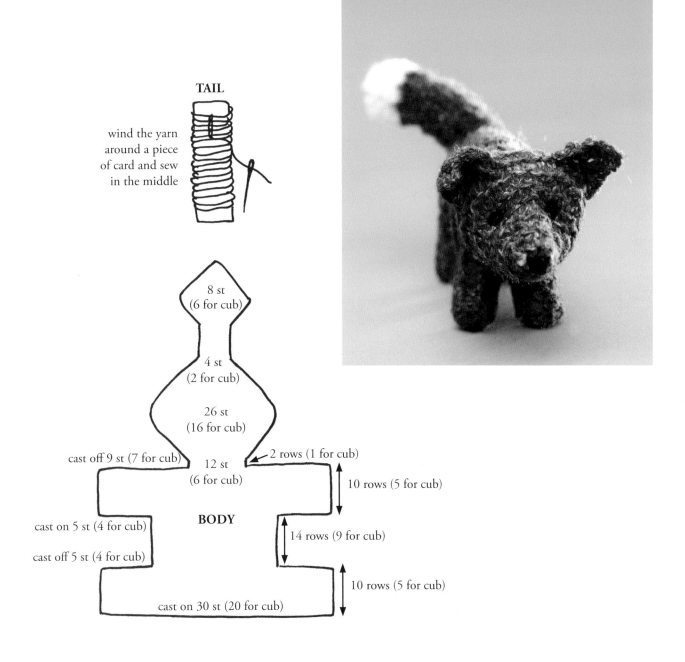

8 st
(6 for cub)

4 st
(2 for cub)

26 st
(16 for cub)

cast off 9 st (7 for cub)   12 st   2 rows (1 for cub)
                             (6 for cub)
                                           10 rows (5 for cub)

BODY

cast on 5 st (4 for cub)   14 rows (9 for cub)

cast off 5 st (4 for cub)

                                           10 rows (5 for cub)

cast on 30 st (20 for cub)

Loooong dog

Materials

- Silk tweed and 2 colours of mohair (maybe choose colours of a dog you know so you can make a look-a-like)
- Black pearl yarn for the eyes, nose and mouth
- Needle size: 3mm (US2–3)
- Carded wool for stuffing

BODY and the head are knitted in one piece. Cast on 36 stitches and work 12 rows in garter stitch. Cast off 7 stitches at the beginning and end of the next row for the back legs (22 stitches). Work 12 rows and cast on 7 stitches at either end of the next row for the front legs. Work 12 rows and cast off 11 stitches at the beginning and end of the next row for the neck. Work 2 rows (14 stitches) for the neck.

HEAD: Knit 5 stitches, increase 1 stitch, knit 2, increase 1 stitch, knit 5. Knit 1 row and repeat increasing on the next row: knit 5 stitches, increase 1 stitch, knit 4, increase 1 stitch, knit 5. Knit 1 row and repeat the same increasing.

NOSE: Knit 1 row and cast on 4 stitches for the nose at the beginning of the next 2 rows, while you carry on increasing twice on every other row at the middle of the work. Keep going until you have 8 rows and 36 stitches. Cast off.

EARS: Cast on 5 stitches and work 2 rows in garter stitch. Increase 1 stitch at the beginning of the next 2 rows (7 stitches). Work 10 rows.

Knit the 2nd and the 3rd stitches together on each row until 1 stitch remains. Break the yarn and pull it through the last stitch.

TAIL: Cast on 8 stitches. Work 5 rows in garter stitch and decrease once in the middle of the work on the next row. Decrease 1 stitch in the middle of the 12th, 22nd and 30th rows. Cast off.

To make up:

Sew the head and the neck together. Sew the legs together as 'tubes' and sew the tummy together. Leave the rear end open for stuffing. You can stuff the legs by stuffing the wool from the paws inwards.

Sew the paws together afterwards. It is important that the dog's legs are nice and firm or it will not stand up.

Sew on the ears. Stuff the tail with wool and sew it on. Sew the eyes and the nose on discreetly. You can also make a 'mouth' for the dog.

Important! If the dog is too wild, you must give him a collar and a lead!

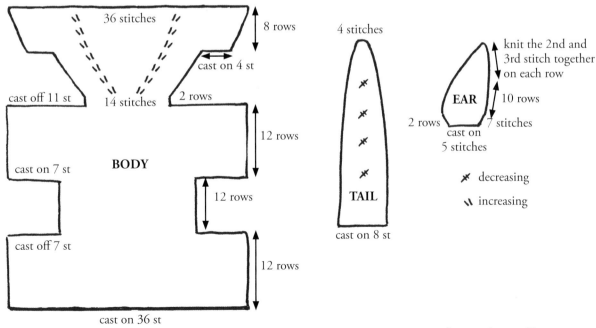

Peter the hedgehog

Materials

- Hedgehog-coloured yarn (a combination of a brownish Shetland wool and two different yarns of raw silk in beige and greeny-brown colours has been used).
- Needle size: to suit yarn used
- Carded wool for stuffing
- The eyes and nose are sewn on in black yarn, e.g. pearl yarn

BODY: cast on 10 stitches and work in stocking stitch. Purl 1 row.

Knit 1 row and start increasing towards the hedgehog's bottom; knit 2 stitches, pick up 1 stitch, knit 1 and pick up 1 stitch, knit 4, pick up 1 stitch, knit 1 and pick up 1 stitch, knit the last 2 stitches (14 stitches). Purl 1 row.

Continue with the same type of increasing on the knit rows with the increased number of stitches: knit 3 stitches, *pick up 1 stitch, knit 1, pick up 1 stitch**, knit 6 stitches and repeat increasing again from * to **. Knit the last 3 stitches. Purl 1 row.

Increase on the next row again, giving 22 stitches in total.

Work 9 rows in stocking stitch, finishing with a purl row.

NOSE: begin decreasing: knit 3 stitches, *knit 2 stitches together, knit 1, knit 2 stitches together**, knit 6 and repeat decreasing from * to **.

Knit the last 3 stitches. Purl 1 row.

Decrease on the next 3 knit rows until 10 stitches left.

Continue decreasing on the knit row: knit 2 stitches together, knit 1, knit 2 stitches together twice, knit 1, knit 2 stitches together. Purl 1 row.

Next row: knit 2 stitches together 3 times. Purl 1 row. Cast off the last 3 stitches.

To make up:

Sew the body together and stuff it with wool until it is firm and the nose is pointed. Sew the spines on with the two raw silk yarns using the rya rug stitch (see facing page). You can cut the loops afterwards.

Sew them in tight rows or in a spiral inwards. Be creative, sewing the eyes and nose with a black yarn.

RYA RUG STITCH is a kind of backwards and forwards stitch, but in this case, make every other stitch into a loop. Don't actually pull the yarn all the way through. The second stitch which is pulled all the way acts as a 'locking' stitch and ensures that the loops cannot be pulled out when you cut them to make spines.

Hedgehogs have a key role in maintaining healthy ecosystems, as they help to control insect populations.
You can make a little hedgehog house in your garden to encourage them to visit.

Pocketmouse

Materials
- Leftover grey yarn, preferably soft and nice to touch, e.g. angora.
- 3mm needles (US2–3)
- 3mm (US D) crochet hook
- Carded wool for stuffing
- Pearl yarn

BODY: cast on 3 stitches.
Increase 3 stitches on the next row, at each end and in the centre.
Purl 1 row and repeat increasing on the knit rows until there are 12 or 15 stitches.
Work 5 rows, finishing with a purl row.
Knit 2 stitches together, knit 1, knit 2 stitches together, knit 1 etc. to the end of the row.
Purl 1 row. On the next row: knit 2 stitches together to the end of the row. Break the yarn and pull it through the last stitch.

To make up:
Sew the mouse together and stuff it with wool until it is firm and hard, otherwise it will easily lose its shape. Crochet a tail of chain stitches.

Sew the ears with 3-4 buttonhole stitches, turn and sew stitches on the top. Continue until the ears are nice and round. Anchor the yarn by sewing into the mouse.
Repeat with the other ear so it is the same as the first.
You can sew the eyes on with some black or grey pearl yarn. If the mouse is white, you can make the eyes red, but that can be a bit scary, so I prefer to make them blue, which is more appealing, as if the sky is reflected in them.

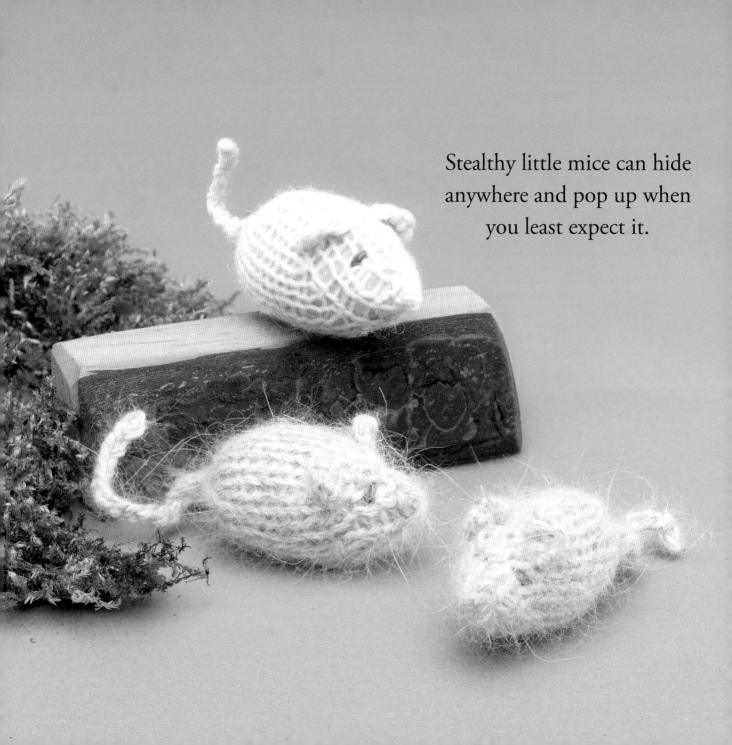

Stealthy little mice can hide
anywhere and pop up when
you least expect it.

Mother pig with piglets

Materials
- Leftover woollen yarns dyed with light madder-red (plant dye) and leftover off-white and pig-pink silk tweed, which together give a good pig-like colour. The pigs are knitted exclusively in garter stitch.
- 3mm (US2–3) needles
- 3mm (US D) crochet hook
- Carded wool for stuffing

Piglets

BODY: cast on 25 stitches and work 6 rows. Cast off 3 stitches at the beginning and end of the next row for the back legs, breaking and rejoining the yarn as necessary (19 stitches). Work 6 rows for the tummy and cast on 3 stitches again at either end of the next row for the front legs (25 stitches). Work 6 rows and cast off 4 stitches at the beginning and end of the next row for the neck (17 stitches).

HEAD: Knit 1 row. Next row: knit 6 stitches, *knit 2 stitches together, knit 1, knit 2 stitches together**, knit 6 (15 stitches). Knit 1 row. Knit 5 stitches and repeat decreasing as before from * to **.

Knit 5 stitches. (13 stitches) Knit 1 row. Repeat until there are 5 stitches left on the needle, 6 times altogether. Remember that there are always 2 stitches less for each decreasing row. Cast off.

EARS: cast on 4 stitches and knit 6 rows. Knit the following rows so that the 2nd and the 3rd stitches are knitted together until 1 stitch remains. Break the yarn and pull it through the last stitch.

Mother pig

BODY: cast on 36 stitches and work 12 rows. Cast off 5 stitches at the beginning and end

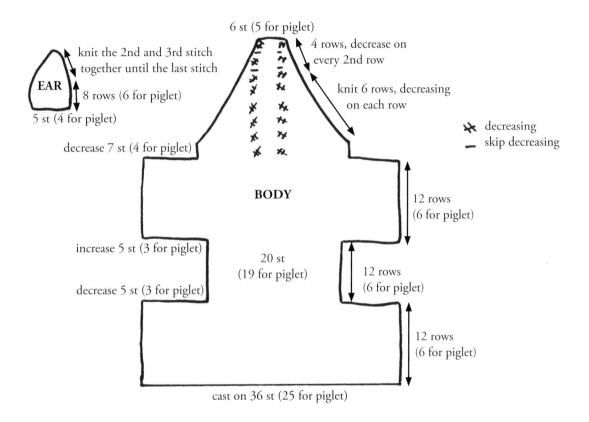

6 st (5 for piglet)

knit the 2nd and 3rd stitch
together until the last stitch

4 rows, decrease on
every 2nd row

EAR

8 rows (6 for piglet)

knit 6 rows, decreasing
on each row

5 st (4 for piglet)

decrease 7 st (4 for piglet)

BODY

✖ decreasing
— skip decreasing

12 rows
(6 for piglet)

increase 5 st (3 for piglet)

20 st
(19 for piglet)

12 rows
(6 for piglet)

decrease 5 st (3 for piglet)

12 rows
(6 for piglet)

cast on 36 st (25 for piglet)

of the next row, breaking and rejoining the yarn as necessary, for the legs (26 stitches). Work 12 rows for the tummy and cast on 5 stitches again at either end of the next row for the front legs (36 st). Work 12 rows and cast off 7 stitches at the beginning and end of the

next row for the neck. (22 st) Work 4 rows. On the following 6 rows: decrease 1 stitch on each side of the centre stitch (2 stitches on each row (10 stitches)). Knit 1 row without decreasing and then repeat decreasing on the following row.

Knit 1 row and repeat decreasing on the next row. Cast off the last 6 stitches.
EARS: cast on 5 stitches and knit 8 rows. Knit the following rows so that the 2nd and 3rd stitches are knitted together until 1 stitch remains. Break the yarn and pull it through the last stitch.

To make up:

Sew the pig's legs together as four 'tubes'. Afterwards sew the tummy, neck and head together. Stuff the pig firmly with wool. It should be solid and firm and ideally give a bit of resistance when you press it. Sew the rear part together and sew the ears firmly so that they point forwards. You can sew the eyes on discreetly. The eyes can enhance the pig's expression, but if you overdo it, it can have the opposite effect and look like a caricature of a pig. Be careful and try it out first. Crochet a tail of chain stitches. You can twist the yarn so the pig's tail curls up nicely.

Glossary

Stitches

Garter Stitch = knit every row
Stocking Stitch = 1 row knit, 1 row purl
Increase = increase by knitting into the front and back of a stitch
Decrease = decrease by knitting 2 stitches together through the back of the stitches (unless otherwise stated in the pattern)
Pick Up 1 Stitch = pick up horizontal loop before the next stitch and knit into the back of it.

Needle sizes

Millimetres	UK no.	US no.
3.0	11	2 to 3
3.5	9 to 10	4
4.0	8	6
4.5	7	7

More books from Hawthorn Press

Making Soft Dolls
Simple Waldorf designs to sew and love
Steffi Stern

From the simplest rag doll to more complex characters, this book gives straight-forward instructions, a guide to buying your materials and upcycling materials you already own. A lovingly hand-made doll makes the perfect present and these dolls will be much loved for generations.

128pp; 200 × 250mm; paperback; ISBN: 978-1-912480-05-0

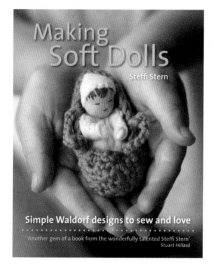

Making Simple Needle Felts
40 Inspiring Seasonal Projects
Steffi Stern

A back-to-basics guide to making needle-felted objects, this book contains chapters on techniques, materials, tools and accessories, as well as projects organised by season. All the projects are suitable for a beginner, with some for little fingers (no needles involved), for beginners, as well as those who have more experience.

176pp; 250 x 200mm; paperback; ISBN: 978-1-907359-97-2

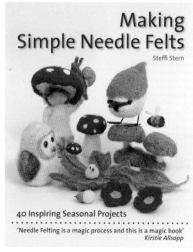

Making Peg Dolls
Over 60 fun, creative projects for children and adults
Margaret Bloom

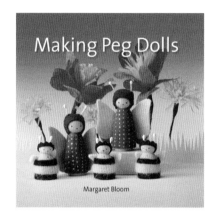

Coming from the Waldorf handcraft tradition, these irresistible dolls encourage creative play and promote the emotional and imaginative development of young children. Easy to follow, step-by-step instructions with beautiful colour illustrations for children and crafters of all levels and experience.

192pp; 200 x 210mm; paperback; ISBN: 978-1-907359-77-4

Making the Children's Year
Seasonal Waldorf Crafts with Children
Marije Rowling

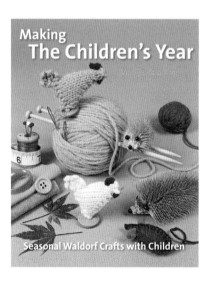

Drawing on the creative ethos of Steiner Waldorf education, this is a full-colour second edition of *The Children's Year*. Packed with all kinds of seasonal crafts, for beginners and experienced crafters, this book is a gift for parents seeking to make toys that will inspire children and provide an alternative to throwaway culture.

240pp; 250 x 200mm; paperback; ISBN: 978-1-907359-69-9

Darning
repair, make, mend
Hikaru Noguchi

This is a book about visible mending, more akin to embroidery and embellishment that will make your favourite clothing even more personal and save it from landfill. Fully illustrated with colour photography throughout, there are step by step images and detailed instructions for projects showing 12 different darning techniques.

96pp; 255 x 186mm; paperback; ISBN: 978-1-912480-15-9

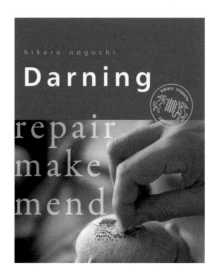

Woodland Crafting
30 projects for children
Patrick Harrison

Woodland Crafting provides the basic knowledge and skills to complete a range of both simple and more advanced craft projects. With beautiful illustrations and detailed instructions, you'll learn to choose your wood, use simple tools, tie knots and develop your own designs to make masks and puppets, torches and arrows, jewellery, ladders, shelters and much more.

96pp; 208 x 198mm; paperback; ISBN: 978-1-912480-83-8

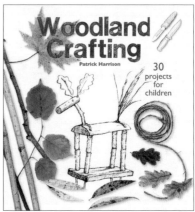

Ordering Books

If you have difficulties ordering Hawthorn Press books from a bookshop, you can order direct from our website **www.hawthornpress.com** or from our UK distributor BookSource: 50 Cambuslang Road, Glasgow, G32 8NB, Tel: (0845) 370 0067, Email: orders@booksource.net. Details of our overseas distributors can be found on our website.

Hawthorn Press